"Children and adults will love these gentle, empowering books. The Learning to Get Along series is a powerful tool for teaching children essential social skills such as empathy, respect, cooperation, and kindness. This straightforward and insightful series helps children visualize how their appropriate behavior positively impacts themselves and others. I heartily recommend this as a solid, classic resource for teaching affective skills to young children."

—**Dr. Stephen R. Covey, Author,** *The 7 Habits of Highly Effective People*

Reach Out and Give

Cheri J. Meiners, M.Ed.

Illustrated by Meredith Johnson

free spirit
PUBLISHING®

Library of Congress Cataloging-in-Publication Data
Meiners, Cheri J., 1957–
    Reach out and give / by Cheri J. Meiners.
        p. cm. — (Learning to get along series)
    ISBN-13: 978-1-57542-204-6
    ISBN-10: 1-57542-204-2
1.   Gratitude—Juvenile literature. 2.   Generosity—Juvenile literature.   I. Title.
    BJ1533.G8M45 2006
    179'.9—dc22
                                                                                    2005033709

Reading Level Grades 1–2; Interest Level Ages 4–8; Fountas & Pinnell Guided Reading Level H

Cover and interior design by Marieka Heinlen
Edited by Marjorie Lisovskis

10 9 8 7
Printed in Hong Kong
P17200711

Free Spirit Publishing Inc.
217 Fifth Avenue North, Suite 200
Minneapolis, MN 55401-1299
(612) 338-2068
help4kids@freespirit.com
www.freespirit.com

Dedication

In grateful memory of my
grandparents Victor, Juanita,
Harold, Rosalina, and Louise
for their sacrifice, kindness,
and generosity
which still make
a difference

Acknowledgments

I wish to thank Meredith Johnson, whose charming illustrations resonate so well with the text, and Marieka Heinlen for the exuberant design. I appreciate Judy Galbraith and the entire Free Spirit family for their dedicated support of the series. I am especially grateful to Margie Lisovskis for her diplomatic style as well as her talented editing. I also recognize Mary Jane Weiss, Ph.D., for her expertise and gift in teaching social skills. Lastly, I thank my fantastic family—David, Kara, Erika, James, Daniel, Julia, and Andrea—who are each an inspiration to me.

The world is beautiful.

There's so much to notice
and be grateful for.

I'm also grateful for people who help me.

There are lots of ways I can show my thanks and give something back.

I want to reach out to people.

I can be generous.

Being generous can take time.

I might help someone without being asked.

Or I might make something
for someone I care about,

or spend some time with that person.

I like to join in and volunteer.

It feels good when I work to make things better.

There are lots of ways to be generous.

I can notice what someone might need or want.

Then I can say and do kind things that might help.

I can share my things, my time, and my talents.

I can help someone smile just by being me and doing things I can do.

When I see a need,

I can sometimes help right away.

At other times, I can get permission first.

I can give service by myself
or with other people.

My little bit can be part of something bigger.

I can reach out to people I know at home, at school, and in my community.

I can even help people I've never met who live in other parts of the world.

My kind act may help one person, or many.

When I give to someone else,
I may need to give up something
for myself.

I think it's worth doing when I imagine how the person might feel.

Giving is like a circle.

Good deeds are
never wasted.

When I do a
favor for someone,

that person might help somebody else.

Kindness may even come back to me.

Being generous brings out the best in me.

And it lifts someone else up.

It helps us get along.

When I do my part,
I can help make the world a better place.

I'm glad that I can make a difference.

Ways to Reinforce the Ideas in *Reach Out and Give*

Reach Out and Give teaches children about being generous and giving service to others. The book introduces beginning concepts of gratitude and helpfulness and of giving time, talent, and things. Here are terms you may want to discuss:

generous: willing to share or give more than is expected

grateful: appreciative or thankful; when you are grateful, you appreciate something and are glad for it

philanthropy: giving time, talent, things, or money to help a person or group

relief: special help for people who need food, water, clothes, shelter, or other basic things

service: something helpful you do for someone else; when you give service, you do something that makes things better for one person or for many people

talents: things a person is able to do especially well

volunteer: to offer to do something helpful without being asked; to reach out to help others because you want to do so

As you read each page spread, ask children:

- What's happening in this picture?

Here are additional questions you might discuss:

Pages 1–3

- What does it mean to be grateful? What are some things you are grateful for? Who are some people you are grateful for?

- What is a way to show someone that you appreciate what the person does?

- Have you ever thanked someone who was kind to you? How did you feel when you thanked the person?

- Has someone ever thanked you for something? How did you feel when that happened?

Pages 4–11

- What does it mean to reach out to other people? *(Discuss this in the context of offering kindness or help without being asked.)* Tell about a time you reached out (or someone reached out to you). What happened?

- What does it mean to be generous? When was a time you were generous (or someone was generous to you)? What did you (the person) do? How did it feel?

- What are some other ways to be generous?

- What is special about doing something for someone without being asked?

- How does making something for someone (spending time with someone) show that you care?

- Tell about a time you or someone in your family volunteered to help with something. What would have happened if no one volunteered to help?

Pages 12–19

- What things do you share? When do you share your time?

- What do you think is one of your talents? What could you do with your talent that might help someone else?

- When are some times someone might need help in our classroom (in our home)? What can you do to help?

- Why is it important to get permission before you give something?

Pages 20–27

- What does it mean to give service?

- *(point to pages 20–21)* What are the people in this picture doing to give service?

- What is a service you can do with other people in our group? With people in your family?

- *(point to pages 22–23)* Who do you think the children are making bags for? How will people use the bags when they receive them?

- What is a way to reach out (give service, be generous) to someone you have never met?

- *(point to pages 24–25)* What are some times to be generous with money (to buy a present, to donate to help people in need)? How is the boy being generous? How do you think his sister will feel when she gets her gift? How will the boy feel? Why?

- What are some good things that can happen when you help someone else?

Pages 28–31

- How do you think being generous helps you get along with other people?

- What are some ways you can make a difference for somebody else?

Generosity Games

Read this book often with your child or group of children. Once children are familiar with the book, refer to it when teachable moments arise involving both positive behavior and problems related to generosity. Make it a point to notice and comment when children willingly offer help or share their time, talent, or things with those around them. In addition, use the following activities to reinforce children's understanding of why and how to reach out and be generous toward others.

"We're Grateful For" Journal

Materials: Large 3-ring binder, 8½" x 11" drawing paper, 3-hole-punched lined writing paper, markers, pencils, paper punch

Preparation: Punch three holes in each sheet of drawing paper. Place the drawing and writing materials in a convenient place for use on a regular basis. Label the binder "We're Grateful For. . . ."

Directions: Talk with children about what it means to be grateful, using discussion questions for pages 1–3 (see page 32). Explain that you will be keeping a *journal*—a daily record—of things everyone is grateful for. Each day, you and the children can each draw a picture or write a journal entry of something you saw, something that happened, or something you realized you are thankful for (such as colorful leaves, a ride to school, a warm sweater). Invite children to date their entries and add them to the book each day. Continue over several weeks, noticing from time to time how full the journal is growing and how much there is to be grateful for.

Words of Appreciation

Have each child in your group write his or her name on a small piece of paper. Place the names in a bag or small box. Draw a different name each day and let several children tell something they appreciate about the child whose name was drawn. Encourage children to mention kind things the person has done, an admirable character trait, or something the person is good at that helps the group. Depending on the size of your group, you may want to draw more than one name each day.

Home or small group variation: Have each person draw another family or group member's name and in turn say something appreciative about the person whose name was drawn. Use this as an ongoing activity to foster gratitude and mutual appreciation.

Extension: As a group, write and illustrate a thank-you letter to a community organization (police department, newspaper, local charity) expressing appreciation and gratitude for the giving the organization does.

Generosity Jar

On small pieces of paper write several ideas of how children might show generosity. Put the ideas in a jar or other container and draw one each day. Have a few children role play the scenario. (See samples below.) Point out that generous acts are done without thought of reward because a person chooses to help. Suggest that children do the act just discussed, or another generous act, in the next day or two (either at school or at home). Follow up each day, inviting children to share their stories of generosity and to role play and discuss new ideas to try.

Sample Scenarios:

- Ask someone to play
- Share a toy or game.
- Pick up trash.
- Help fold laundry.
- Find something nice to say.
- Make a thank-you note.
- Visit a friend and take a treat.
- Help someone with a math problem.
- Help someone pick up blocks or art supplies.

Service Cards

On 3" x 5" index cards, have or help children write a service they will do for another child or a family member. ("I'll read you a story." "I'll take out the trash." "I'll pick up the art supplies with you." "I'll help you clean your desk.") Have children draw the name of a child and do the service sometime during the week. Children can give the card to the child the day they plan to do the service, or can put it where it will be found as a surprise. Follow up with discussions of how it felt to help someone, how it felt to be helped, and why doing service for others helps people get along. If you wish, continue each week, having children offer a different service and choose the name of a different child.

Giving Tree

Materials: Bulletin board, colored construction paper, scissors, stapler

Create a Giving Tree with branches to hold many leaves. Cut out paper leaves, several for each child. Explain to children that the Giving Tree lets everyone notice acts of kindness and generosity. When a child sees someone do something generous, the child can write or dictate a description of the kindness on a leaf and add the leaf to the board.

Making a Difference Together

Review and discuss what it means to volunteer and give service to others. Then talk about a way that your class or family group could work together to fill a need in your school or community. Begin by identifying a group (senior citizens, soldiers, those who are homeless) or an area (a park, library, playground) in need of help or improvement. Then think together of a way to work together to make a difference. Discuss children's ideas, using questions such as: "Why is this a good project for lots of us to do together?" "Who would this help?" "How would it help?" Enlist the aid of other adults to support children in giving service.

Sample Ideas for Giving Service:

- Visit and read with children at a hospital.
- Get pledges for reading or doing math to benefit a charity.
- Collect canned goods for a food bank.
- Send a box of books or snacks to soldiers.
- Make a quilt or blanket for a hospital or shelter.
- Visit and play games with people in a senior center or nursing home.
- Collect and donate money for disaster victims.
- Collect used eyeglasses for an eye bank.
- Make hygiene kits for a shelter.
- Take part in a toy or clothing drive.
- Raise money or collect packaged food for an animal shelter.
- Plant spring bulbs at a park.
- Make posters for a recycling drive.
- Pick up litter along a public street or on a playground.

Free Spirit's Learning to Get Along® Series

Help children learn, understand, and practice basic social and emotional skills. Real-life situations, diversity, and concrete examples make these read-aloud books appropriate for childcare settings, schools, and the home. *Each book: 40 pp., color illust., S/C, 9" x 9", ages 4–8.*

ACCEPT AND VALUE EACH PERSON
Introduces diversity and related concepts: respecting differences, being inclusive, and appreciating people just the way they are.

BE CAREFUL AND STAY SAFE
Teaches children how to avoid potential dangers, ask for help, follow directions, use things carefully, and plan ahead.

BE HONEST AND TELL THE TRUTH
Children learn that being honest in words and actions builds self-confidence and trust, and that telling the truth can take courage and tact.

BE POLITE AND KIND
Introduces children to good manners and gracious behavior including saying "Please," "Thank you," "Excuse me," and "I'm sorry."

COOL DOWN AND WORK THROUGH ANGER
Teaches skills for working through anger: self-calming, getting help, talking and listening, apologizing, and viewing others positively.

JOIN IN AND PLAY
Teaches the basics of cooperation, getting along, making friends, and being a friend.

KNOW AND FOLLOW RULES
Shows children that following rules can help us stay safe, learn, be fair, get along, and instill a positive sense of pride.

LISTEN AND LEARN
Introduces and explains what listening means, why it's important to listen, and how to listen well.

REACH OUT AND GIVE
Begins with the concept of gratitude; shows children contributing to their community in simple yet meaningful ways.

RESPECT AND TAKE CARE OF THINGS
Children learn to put things where they belong and ask permission to use things. Teaches simple environmental awareness.

SHARE AND TAKE TURNS
Gives reasons to share; describes four ways to share; points out that children can also share their knowledge, creativity, and time.

TALK AND WORK IT OUT
Peaceful conflict resolution is simplified so children can learn to calm down, state the problem, listen, and think of and try solutions.

TRY AND STICK WITH IT
Introduces children to flexibility, stick-to-it-iveness (perseverance), and the benefits of trying something new.

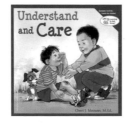

UNDERSTAND AND CARE
Builds empathy in children; guides them to show they care by listening to others and respecting their feelings.

WHEN I FEEL AFRAID
Helps children under-stand their fears; teaches simple coping skills; encourages children to talk with trusted adults about their fears.

LEARNING TO GET ALONG® SERIES INTERACTIVE SOFTWARE
Children follow along or read on their own, using a special highlight feature to click or hear word definitions. User's Guide included. *For Mac and Windows.*

www.freespirit.com • 800.735.7323

Volume discounts: edsales@freespirit.com
Speakers bureau: speakers@freespirit.com